See for Yourself

SHOPS

Jeff Stanfield

WAYLAND

Homes ● School ● Shops ● The Street ● Transport

HOW TO USE THIS BOOK

This book will help you find out about shops. All the questions highlighted in **bold** have answers on pages 26–27, but try to work them out for yourself first. Investigate the shops near you by trying some of the detective activities on pages 28–29. You'll find difficult words explained on page 30.

Most of the photographs in this book were taken in Leeds and Bradford. So you can compare the different shops in Leeds and Bradford with the shops near your own home.

Series editor: Polly Goodman
Book editor: Mike Hirst
Book designer: Jean Wheeler
Cover design: Dome Design

British Library Cataloguing in Publication Data
Stanfield, Jeff
    Shops. – (See For Yourself)
    1. Stores, Retail – England – Bradford – Juvenile literature
    2. Stores, Retail – England – Bradford – Problems, exercises, etc.
    – Juvenile literature
    I. Title
    381.1'0942817

ISBN 0 7502 1953 X

Typeset by Jean Wheeler, England
Printed and bound in Italy by G. Canale & C.S.p.A., Turin

First published in 1997 by
Wayland Publishers Ltd
61 Western Road,
Hove, East Sussex
BN3 1JD, England

© Copyright 1997 Wayland Publishers Ltd

Find Wayland on the internet at
http://www.wayland.co.uk

Photographic credits
All the photographs in this book, except those listed below, were taken by Bipinchandra J. Mistry.
Cover: *calculator, money and purse*: Chapel Studios; *children and shopping basket*: Wayland Picture Library. Pages 5 (bottom), 19 (bottom), 25 (top): Wayland Picture Library.

CONTENTS

SHOPPING AROUND

There are lots of different types of shops. You can find shops in cities, towns and villages.

Most people have a shop near their home.

◀ This shop sells newspapers to the people who live nearby.

Look at signs outside the shop.

What else does the shop sell?

Which type of shop is nearest to your home?

◄ Sometimes there are different shops in a row called a parade.

Why is it helpful to have several different shops in one place?

Town and city centres have lots of big shops.

**How can you tell ►
what this shop sells?**

Sometimes you find shops in unusual places.

◄ This shop is on a farm.
It sells fresh fish from the farm's ponds.

MARKET STALLS

Many years ago, outdoor markets were the only place to buy things.

Today, some people still enjoy shopping at open markets. Markets are often busy and colourful.

▲ The stallkeepers put up their stalls in the market-place.
They start work early in the morning.

Markets often sell many different things besides food.

What can you buy at ▶ these stalls?

Some markets are held indoors. ▼

▲ This indoor market has a beautiful hall with a glass roof.

Why is the roof made of glass?

Why are indoor markets a good idea?

Is there a market near your home?

LOCAL SHOPS

Local shops are often on a corner or in a parade.

Corner shops are usually small, but they sell lots of different things. Many stay open late.

▲ This man is buying a drink and some sweets from his local corner shop.

◀ This shop is really two shops in one!
It sells newspapers, but it is a grocery shop too.
You can buy food here.

What job does the boy do?
Why does he have a bicycle?

Local shops are ▶ friendly places.

This greengrocer knows his customers. They have a chat.

The shop sells fruit and vegetables.

Look at the shop window.

What else does the shop sell?

CITY SHOPPING

In large towns and cities, Saturday is a busy day for shops.

Some people ▶ travel to the city centre in cars, but buses are often the best way of getting there.

Why are buses a better type of transport than cars in a city centre?

◀ Big shops have special signs, called logos, to show people where they are.

What does the logo for C&A look like?

▲ Many towns and cities have streets called pedestrian precincts.

Cars and lorries are not allowed to enter these streets.

Why are pedestrian precincts good for shoppers?

PEDESTRIAN
ZONE

Except for
loading
M'night-10.30am
4.30pm-M'night
and
parking bays
only

At any
time

DEPARTMENT STORES

Most towns have department stores.

You can buy almost anything in a department store.

▲ This department store is so big that it stretches across two buildings.

◀ At the entrance to the store there is a store guide.

What does the guide tell shoppers?

Which floor sells beds?

DEBENHAMS STORE GUIDE

FIFTH FLOOR	
Clearance	Toilets

THIRD FLOOR	
Beds	Customer Accounts
Parent & Baby Room.	Toilets

SECOND FLOOR	
Bath Accessories	Toys
China & Glass	Toilets
Coffee Shop	Linens
Curtains	Toilets
Toys	

FIRST FLOOR	
Womenswear	Knitwear
Coats & Raincoats	Principles
Blouses	Suits
Coats & Raincoats	Underwear
Dresses	

THIS FLOOR GROUND	
Accessories	Shoes
Jewellery	Skirts
Cosmetics	Swim Wear
Dorothy Perkins	Top Shop
Young Fashion	Top Man

LOWER GROUND	
Menswear	Principles for Men
Champion sports	Shirts
Coats & Raincoats	Suits & Jackets
Luggage	Childrenswear
Underwear	Trousers

12

Inside the store there are lots of different counters. They display all the items that are for sale.

In this part of the shop you ▶ can buy make-up and clothes.

Shoppers choose what they want to buy.

◀ They pay for the goods at a special counter called a pay zone.

SHOPPING MALLS

◀ This round building used to be a place where farmers sold corn. Today it is used as a shopping mall.

▲ A shopping mall is a large building with lots of different shops inside.

◀ Some malls have cafés and restaurants too, where shoppers can stop for a drink or lunch.

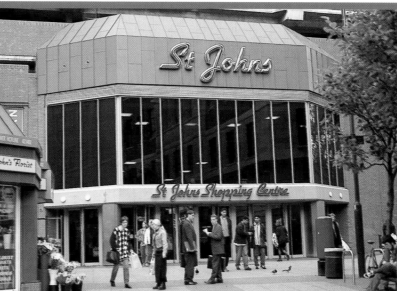

▲ Compare this shopping mall with the one on the opposite page.

How are they different?

◀ There are three ways of getting from one floor to another inside.

What are they?

OUT OF TOWN

Nowadays, there are large shopping centres on the edges of towns and cities.

These big, modern buildings are called superstores.

At the entrance to this shopping centre there is a sign. It tells you which way to go for the different shops.

This shopping centre has some other things besides shops.

What are they?

16

People travel to out-of-town shopping centres in cars or buses. There is a big car park next to each superstore.

◀ This woman has been shopping for food.

Why is it easy for her to shop at this shopping centre?

How has this ▶ shopping centre made its car park look attractive?

SUPERMARKETS

Most people buy a lot of ▶ their food in a supermarket.

As you walk around a supermarket, you choose the food you want and put it in a trolley or a basket.

▼ At this counter, people ask the assistant for pieces of cheese and cold meat.

◀ The woman in the black coat is taking a ticket with a number on it.

What is it for?

▲ Shoppers pay for their food at the check-out.

Every packet of food has a bar code. ▶
A computer at the check-out reads
the pattern of black lines.

The bar code tells the computer how much that
packet of food costs. The computer adds up the bill.

Do you ever go to a supermarket?
What is it called?

SHOPS ON WHEELS

Mobile shops move around from place to place.

◀ These girls are buying ice creams. The ice-cream van has parked outside their school.

How do you know if there is an ice-cream van nearby?

A burger van ▶ can travel wherever there are lots of people. This one is at a market.

Where else might you see a burger van?

▲ Milk floats are another type of mobile shop. They carry milk to people's homes.

Early each morning, this milkman ▶ puts milk on people's doorsteps.

Milk floats have a special electric engine. The engine is very quiet.

Why do milk floats have quiet engines?

HOME SHOPPING

You can buy things without going into a shop.

This man is ▶ delivering a mail-order catalogue.

◀ You can look at mail-order catalogues at home.

People choose what they want to buy. Then they order what they want by phone, or by writing a letter.

Have you ever looked inside a mail-order catalogue?

▲ This man is watching a shopping channel on television. It shows items that are for sale.

Where is the phone number to call if you want to buy something?

You can look at a toy-shop ▶ catalogue on this computer.

In some countries you can now use a computer to order food from a supermarket.

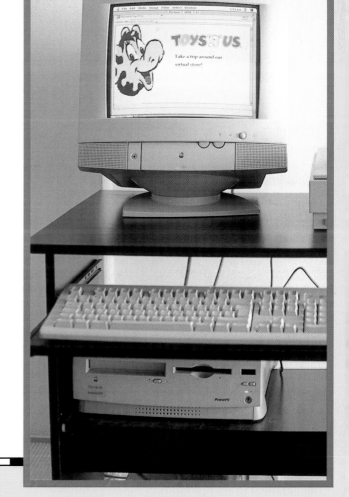

SHOPPING ON THE MOVE

People often need to buy things when they are travelling.

Most big railway stations have shops, like this newsagents. ▶

This station also has a machine that takes people's photographs.

◀ This garage sells petrol, but you can also buy drinks, newspapers, flowers and other items.

Why does the garage sell drinks, newspapers and flowers?

People on long journeys often need to buy some food quickly to eat on the way.

Many railway and bus stations have fast-food restaurants.

Why are hamburgers called fast food? ▶

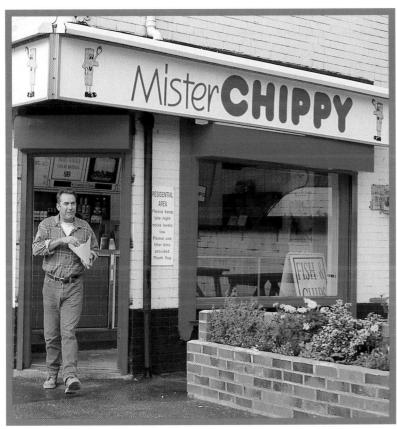

In Britain, fish and chips are a popular type of fast food.

◀ You often see people eating fish and chips as they walk along the street.

What is your favourite type of fast food? Where do you buy it?

ANSWERS TO QUESTIONS

Pages 4–5 Shopping Around

The shop sells tickets for the national lottery. You can also make photocopies in the shop.

It is helpful to have several different shops in one place so you can buy lots of things without having to travel very far.

You can tell the shop sells clothes because they are displayed in the windows.

Pages 6–7 Market Stalls

You can buy clothes at these stalls.

The roof is made of glass so that plenty of light can get into the market.

Indoor markets are a good idea because the market stalls are safe from the wind and the rain.

Pages 8–9 Local Shops

The boy delivers newspapers. He uses his bicycle to go from house to house.

A sign in the window says that the shop also sells fresh fish.

Pages 10–11 City Shopping

If everyone drives to the city centre in a car, there is too much traffic. It is difficult to park. Cars get stuck in traffic jams and the air gets polluted.

The logo for C&A has white letters on a blue background. The logo also has a red, wavy border and rainbow-coloured stripes.

Pedestrian precincts are safe places for shoppers. There is no need to watch out for cars and lorries.

Pages 12–13 Department Stores

The guide tells shoppers where to find the different items that are for sale. Beds are on the third floor.

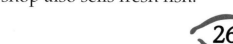

26

Pages 14–15 Shopping Malls

The shopping mall on page 14 is in an old building. St John's Shopping Centre, on page 15, is in a modern building. It was specially built to be a new shopping mall.

Shoppers go from one floor to another by using the stairs, the escalator, or one of the glass lifts.

Pages 16–17 Out of Town

The shopping centre has a burger restaurant, a library and a special place for disabled drivers to park their cars.

The woman can drive to the superstore in her car and park right outside. She takes her shopping out of her trolley and loads it straight into her car.

This shopping centre has planted trees, flowers and bushes in the car park next to the superstores.

Pages 18–19 Supermarkets

The ticket lets the woman know when it is her turn to be served. She waits until her number lights up above the counter.

Pages 20–21 Shops on Wheels

Ice-cream vans usually ring a loud bell or play a tune when they enter a street. People can hear the ice-cream van even if they are indoors.

Milk floats have quiet engines because they drive through the streets very early in the morning. If they had loud engines, they would wake people up.

Pages 22–23 Home Shopping

The phone number is at the bottom of the television screen.

Pages 24–25 Shopping on the Move

The garage sells drinks, newspapers, flowers and other goods because people often become thirsty on journeys. If people are travelling to visit friends, they might want to buy flowers to give as a present. Garages are also useful shops for people travelling home from work. They can buy bread or milk as well as petrol.

Hamburgers are called fast food because they do not take long to cook. They are ready in a few minutes.

DETECTIVE ACTIVITIES

You can have lots of fun finding out about the shops near your home. Try these activities and see if you are a good shop detective. But remember, always ask an adult to help you if you are doing detective work out of doors!

● Draw a picture map of the route to your nearest corner shop.

● Keep a record of the different shops you and your family visit in one week. Draw a picture of each shop, and write down how many times you visited it.

● It is your birthday. You can buy ten different presents from ten different shops. Write down what your shopping list will be.

● When you go to a market, look at the stalls. How many different kinds can you find?

● Ask an adult to help you take a small cassette recorder to a market. Record the different sounds you can hear there. Play the cassette to your friends. Can they recognize the sounds?

● Ask an adult to help you make a survey of who uses a corner shop near your home. Stand outside the shop for fifteen minutes, and ask the shoppers where they live. Mark their homes on a map of your area. Do some people come from far away?

● Every month, make a list of what is for sale in your local fruit and vegetable shop. Do the fruit and vegetables change from month to month?

● Most greengrocers put boxes of fruit and vegetables outside their shops. They look very colourful. Draw a colour diagram to show how the greengrocer sets out the different fruit and vegetables.

● Make drawings of the logos of shops where you go shopping. Show the logos to your family or a friend. Do they know what each shop sells?

● Make up your own imaginary department store. What will it sell? Draw a store guide to tell people where they can find the different items for sale.

● If you visit a shopping mall, try to pick up two maps of the mall. Then you can play 'Hunt the Shop' with a friend. Look at the list of shops and choose one. See if your friend can find it on the map. Then ask your friend to give you a shop to find.

● Draw a picture of your favourite shop. What does it sell? What sign does it have on the outside?

● Make a speaking map. If you have a small cassette recorder, take it with you next time you go to a shopping centre. On your way there, record where you go and what buildings you see.

● Make a model of a shopping centre near your home. Use old matchboxes for the shops. You can make superstores out of old cereal packets.

● When you next go to a supermarket, look at all the different jobs people are doing. Draw a big picture, showing as many different supermarket jobs as you can and where they take place.

● When you get home from the supermarket, look at the labels on the food you have bought. Where do different foods come from? Mark the places on a map of the world.

● Make a plan of your local supermarket. Show the positions of the different kinds of food.

● Watch out for mobile shops in your area. How many do you see in one week? What do they sell?

● Ask an adult for an old catalogue. Cut out the pictures of your favourite items. Then stick them into a scrapbook to make your own catalogue.

● What do you need if you go on a long train journey? Make a list. Next time you visit a railway station, look in the station shops. How many of the items can you find for sale there?

DIFFICULT WORDS

Bar code A pattern of black lines that gives information such as price to a computer.

Catalogue A book that shows things you can buy.

Check-out The place where you pay in a supermarket or superstore.

Corner shops Small shops in housing areas. Corner shops are often on street corners, and they sell many different items.

Department stores Large shops. They sell many different items.

Fast food Food that is quick to cook, like hamburgers or fish and chips.

Greengrocer Someone who sells fruit and vegetables.

Logo A sign or a symbol that is a special way of writing a name.

Mail order A type of shopping that uses the post. The shopper orders items by letter or over the telephone. The goods are sent to the shopper by post.

Market-place A piece of land where a market is held.

Out-of-town shopping centres Shops that are built on the edge of a town or city.

Parade A row of shops.

Pay zone The place where you pay in a department store.

Pedestrian precincts Streets where people are only allowed to go on foot.

Shopping centre A place with several different shops.

Shopping mall A large building with many shops under one roof.

Stalls Big tables or benches, usually with covers. At a market, goods are displayed on stalls.

Store guide A sign that shows where to go to buy different items in a large store.

Superstores Very large shops or supermarkets.

Transport A way of moving goods or people from one place to another. Cars are a type of transport.

Other Books to Read

Mapwork 1 by David Flint and Mandy Suhr (Wayland, 1992)

Mapwork 2 by Julie Warne and Mandy Suhr (Wayland, 1992)

My First Look at Shopping (Dorling Kindersley, 1991)

Shopkeeper by Jane Shuter (Heinemann, 1996)

Shopping by Stewart Ross (Wayland, 1993)

Shopping for Food by Ruth Thomson (Watts Books, 1992)

Shops and Markets Around the World by Godfrey Hall (Wayland, 1995)

Stepping through History: Shops and Markets by Peggy Burns (Wayland, 1995)

INDEX

Page numbers in **bold** show that there is a photograph as well as information on the page.